The Nature of Friendship

THE NATURE OF
Friendship

MARYJO KOCH

**Andrews McMeel
Publishing, LLC**

Kansas City

Concept and Design: Jennifer Barry Design, Fairfax, California
Production Assistance: Kristen Hall

10 11 12 13 WKT 10 9 8 7 6 5 4 3 2

ISBN-13: 978-0-7407-7952-7

ISBN-10: 0-7407-7952-4

Library of Congress Control Number: 2008931671

www.andrewsmcmeel.com

Attention: Schools and Businesses

Andrews McMeel books are available at quantity discounts with
bulk purchase for educational, business, or sales promotional use.
For information, please write to:
Special Sales Department, Andrews McMeel Publishing, LLC,
1130 Walnut Street, Kansas City, Missouri 64106.

*F*riendships are everywhere in nature. We all need each other—every one of us.

Nature's friendships are revealed in the way creatures cooperate to help each other survive: giving shelter and food, defending the other's life, or just being in physical contact—like two fish "kissing."

I love to watch California Quail. There is always one bird that acts as a sentry for the rest of the covey to make sure everyone is safe. With honeybees and bumblebees, the colonies thrive and grow because the older generations of sisters feed and raise the younger generations. Ant colonies operate on a similar kind of mutual support.

Watch a hummingbird sipping the nectar of a flower; these are two entirely different species that need each other to survive. As the flower feeds the hummingbird, the hummingbird leaves behind pollen to fertilize the flower, so it can make seeds. The Clown Fish takes shelter within the Sea Anemone's stinging tentacles and raises its young there. The fish's activity stirs the water around its host, helping the Sea Anemone stay healthy.

What's true in nature is also true in our lives: every one of us needs friends of all kinds. May these natural relationships inspire the friendships in your life!

—Maryjo Koch

Tried & True

A good friend is hard to find.

I

A true friend overlooks your thorns to admire your flowers.

To love and
be loved by a friend is
to feel the sun from
both sides.

It takes
a long time to
hatch an
old friend.

A true friend
is someone who thinks
you're a good egg
even though she knows
you're a little
cracked.

A friend is someone you want to be around when you feel like being alone.

True friends
are always together
in spirit.

Friendship doubles our joy and divides our grief.

A friend is someone who knows what you're saying, even if you're not talking.

Good friends
can see through you
and still
enjoy the show!

Making Friends

More friends are made with honey than with vinegar.

II

There are no strangers, only

friends you haven't met yet.

We don't *make*
our friends—
we recognize
them.

Be careful
of friends
who take
and never give.

You can't
eat your friends
and
have them too!

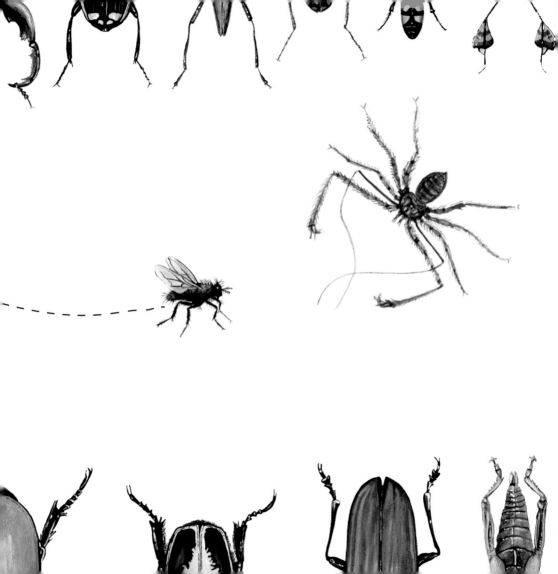

A friend is
someone who is there
for you when she could
be somewhere else.

It's okay to
ask friends for help.
It shows you
really trust them.

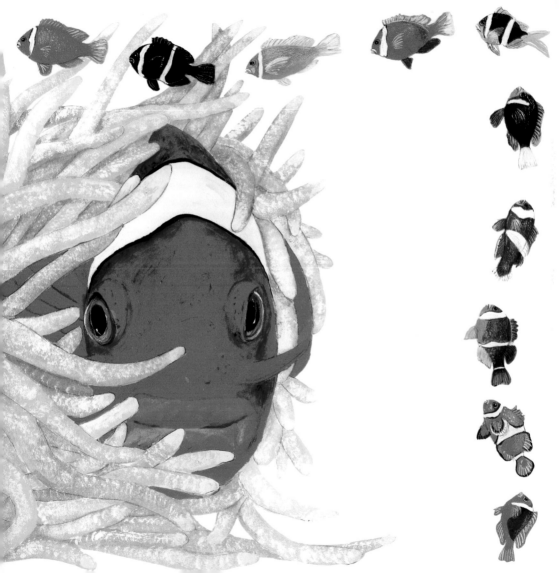

There are many
different types
of friends,

but a true friend
always likes you for
who you are.

Things that
attract and bug you
about your friends can help
you to understand
who you are.

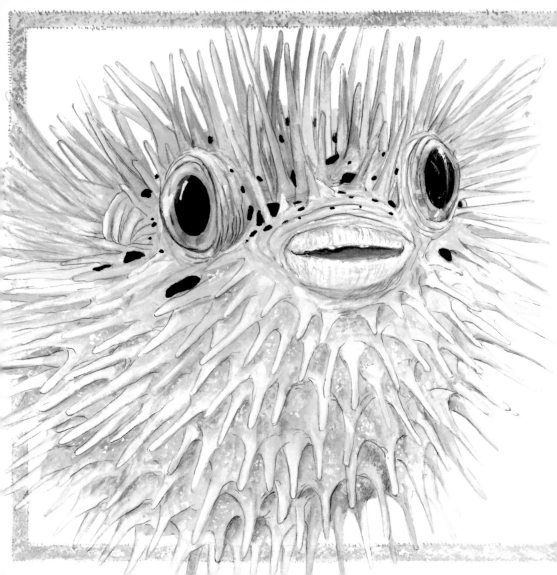

Even pals who are
prickly
can still be friends.

Friends who are flexible

are more fun to be with.

Laughter is the shortest distance between two friends.

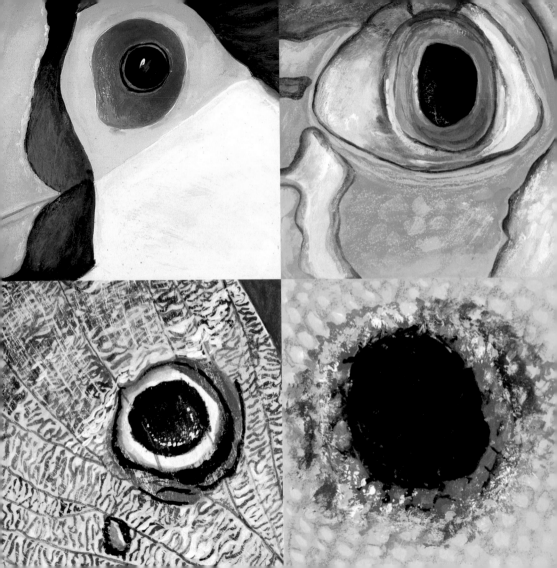

Good friends help us
see things
from a new perspective.

Friends & Family

Friends are relatives we make for ourselves.

III

Nature gives you
your family,
but you get to choose
your friends.

ten thousand relatives.

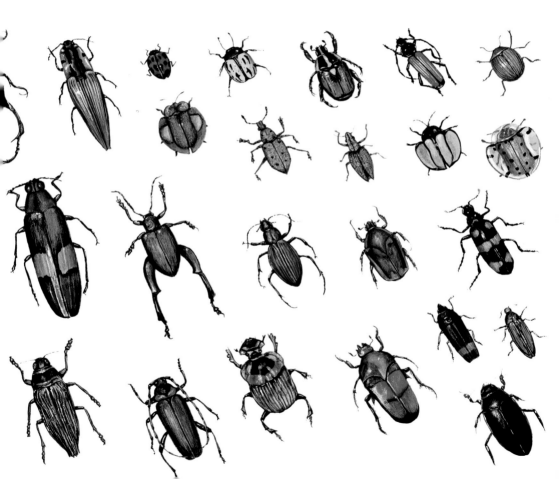

A circle of friends

makes us
feel like part of
the gang.

Similarities make friendships fun. Differences make them more interesting.

Shared experience is the food of all friendships.

Good friends let you
branch out
in many directions
without growing
apart.

A friend is
someone who always
makes you feel
comfortable.

Friendship
is an endless
garden
of surprises
in which
we bloom.

About Friends

Rose
One of the loveliest and sweetest smelling of all flowers is as appealing to plant-eating animals as it to humans. So to ensure survival, roses developed thorns on their stems and branches to make it difficult for animals to take a bite without a painful lesson. For humans as well as animals, admiring the flowers of the rosebush goes hand in hand with avoiding its thorns.

Sunflowers
Exemplifying the phenomenon known as compound inflorescence, each sunflower blossom is actually a cluster of hundreds of smaller flowers. Each individual floret has its own reproductive apparatus and produces a single seed. Sunflowers got their name because they follow the sun's course across the sky by rotating their blossom heads toward the sun from dawn to dusk. Chemicals in the flowers are attracted to the sun's rays.

Nesting Anna's Hummingbirds
Because hummingbirds must spend a lot of their time finding and feeding on flower nectar, they are for the most part unsociable. In fact, they are often described as being pugnacious or feisty since they chase away competitors to defend their food territories. Male and female hummingbirds do not form a pair-bond after mating; the female is left to care for eggs and chicks by herself. But hummingbirds are important friends and pollinators to a variety of flowers. Some with unusual bill shapes have even coevolved with individual flower species.

Common Eider Hatchling
The shell of a bird's egg has to be strong enough to bear the weight of a nesting parent, yet not so hard and thick that the grown hatchling cannot break its way out. After hatching, Common Eider ducklings leave the nest within twenty-four hours; they feed themselves as they learn to dive within one hour of entering the water.

California Sister Butterflies on Summer Borage

Adult California Sister butterflies are found in oak woodlands and usually feed on fruit that has fallen from its source or has been pecked by birds. The butterflies also feed on the salt and mineral-rich water at the edges of mud puddles, but like hummingbirds and bees, they will occasionally sip nectar from flowers. They are the last butterflies of the late summer/fall season before the frost of winter comes.

Tropical Fish

Survival in the sea requires strict economy: every act and feature of every life-form serves a purpose. If the riot of colors found in the deep offered no advantage, then natural selection or random genetic drift would erase the bold hues. Conspicuous color signals availability for mating; it also helps define territorial boundaries and confuse predators. Brilliantly colored fish can easily hide from their enemies in the colorful reefs they inhabit, which gives them ample ecological justification for their ostentatious appearance.

Sea Horses

With its horse-shaped head and monkey-like tail, the sea horse is one of the strangest and most appealing creatures that inhabit our coral reefs. It feeds upright continuously throughout the day using its prehensile tail to grasp the coral as it slurps down shellfish or whole baby fish. And during courtship, these shy and peaceful creatures entwine their tails and dance together.

Ostriches

The ostrich is the largest and strongest of all birds. Although a flightless bird, it can run at great speeds (up to 50 mph) and has excellent eyesight and acute hearing. Ostriches usually travel in small flocks of five or six but have also been seen in groups of up to fifty members. The ostrich is an extremely wary bird—its height and keen senses make it an excellent sentry, and it can rarely be approached by predators within one hundred yards in the open.

Jellyfish

Jellyfish have taken many forms in response to varied environments. Those jellyfish that call the dark, midwater depths home wear coats of many colors, while many from the sunlit surface are nearly transparent. Some jellyfish are avid swimmers while others drift with the currents, feeding and getting their energy from plankton, fish, and photosynthetic organisms that live inside their cells.

Honeybees

Bees are some of the most social of all insects, forming colonies whose members gather nectar from flowers to make their special food known as honey. Bees suck the nectar into a special honey sac in their abdomens where enzymes digest the natural sugars. After depositing the product in wax honeycomb cells, bees fan it with their wings to speed the evaporation of excess moisture. The reduced liquid, eaten by both larvae and mature bees, is honey.

Kissing Gourami Fish

Fish sometimes find it difficult to determine if another member of their own species is male or female, but when kissing gouramis begin their ritualistic displays, they reveal their genders in due course. Male gouramis will occasionally challenge each other by locking mouths in what looks like kissing; however, the "kissing" itself is never harmful.

Rajah Brooke's Birdwing Butterflies

Native to the rain forests of Borneo and Malaysia, these large butterflies are easily identified by their bold black and iridescent green tooth-shaped markings and bright red heads. In the perpetually warm, damp climate of the rain forest, the world's largest plants are pollinated by some of the world's largest insects like these birdwings, whose wingspan can reach seven inches. They are powerful flyers and often travel in groups as they feed on fruit juices and flower nectar in the forest canopy.

Venus Flytrap and Bees
Not all plants are friendly to their airborne neighbors. Carnivorous plants like the Venus Flytrap supplement their photosynthetic diet by feeding on insects. Set off by an alighting victim, trigger hairs on the plant slam its hinged leaf lobes shut. Inside, digestive enzymes dissolve the prey.

Whip Spider, Beetle Legs, and Fly
Tropical Whip Spiders are one of the few species of arachnids that show signs of social behavior. Mother Whip Spiders comfort their young with their feelers, and young siblings are in constant tactile contact with each other. However, like all spiders, they prey on other insects, using their whips as sensory probes to locate food. These very thin whip-like legs can extend several times the length of their bodies in many directions. They have no silk glands or venomous fangs, but they use prominent pincer-like pedipalps to capture their prey.

California Quail Chicks
California Quails are very sociable birds that often gather in small flocks known as coveys. Their nests are shallow scrapes in the ground lined with vegetation and camouflaged under a shrub or other ground cover. The female quail usually lays around twelve eggs. Once the babies hatch, they associate with both parents and the other chicks. Often, quail families group together into communal broods that include at least two females, multiple males, and many offspring.

Desert Tortoise and Greater Roadrunner
These are two desert dwellers that move at very different speeds. The desert tortoise shuffles along at .13 to .3 miles per hour, while Roadrunners can run at speeds of up to 18.5 miles per hour and generally prefer sprinting to flying. Although capable of flight, the Greater Roadrunners are terrestrial cuckoos that spend most of their time on the ground. They will fly to escape faster-moving predators such as coyotes, but the tortoises have to spend much of their time burrowed underground to escape predators and extreme desert temperatures.

Clown Fish and Sea Anemone

Sea Anemones and Clown Fish live in perfect harmony on the coral reef. To protect itself from the Sea Anemone's deadly sting, the Clown Fish wears "grease paint" of slimy mucus, as the Sea Anemone does to protect itself from its own stinging tentacles. In exchange for the safe haven it offers the Clown Fish, the Sea Anemone nibbles on whatever food the fish drops. And some species of fish are lured by the Clown Fish's bright costume only to become food themselves for the immobile Sea Anemone.

Grasshoppers

Known for their powerful back legs, grasshoppers and their relatives—crickets, cicadas, and katydids—can vault skyward with a slingshot leap and keep continuously aloft for thousands of miles on leathery wings. Some species of grasshopper such as locusts have both solitary and gregarious (swarm) phases when they form large groups to migrate and feed. Others, like the Bush-Hopper Grasshopper, native to Africa, travel in small swarms and flash their brightly colored wings or change to camouflage coloring when threatened.

Bugs on Leaves

Like all animals, insects need to communicate. Noise, scent, movement, and color are all employed by the insect world to attract and warn other insects or predators. Depending on the beholder's point of view, each species' unique characteristics are either appealing or alarming, but are all part of the seemingly infinite and amazing world of nature.

Puffer Fish and Porcupinefish

Sometimes called the hedgehogs of the sea, puffers and porcupinefish can raise their spines from a flattened resting position to make a prickly mouthful for potential predators. When startled, the fish blows itself up like a balloon by swallowing water or air. Inflating its body increases its inedibility, for when it doubles or triples in size it can be too much to swallow. When two puffers or porcupines meet to dispute territorial boundaries, they will puff out and flip belly up, displaying a brilliant white underside that exaggerates their size even more.

Blue Sea Stars

Built of calcareous plates or ossicles, the sea star's light, strong, and extremely flexible skeleton is a miracle of biological engineering. Interweaving living tissue with its honeycomb skeleton, the echinoderm shows off skin that glows within the colorful calcium carbonate plates and spines, each consisting of a single crystal. The highly maneuverable spikes project from conical muscles in the sea star's body wall. The underside of the sea star features tiny hydraulic tube feet, and these suckered appendages enable it to crawl across the ocean floor.

Tawny Frogmouth and Laughing Kookaburra (shown left)

These two birds have a lot in common. They are both carnivorous eaters, have unique calls, are similar in size (around 16 inches), and are natives of Australia and New Guinea. The loud, hysterical laughter of the Laughing Kookaburra is so distinctive that filmmakers often add it to the soundtracks of jungle scenes, even though this kingfisher is found solely in the savanna woodlands of Australia. The Tawny Frogmouth is a nocturnal bird with a reverberating booming call.

Eyes and Eyespots

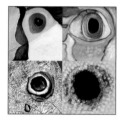

(left to right, top to bottom: Toucan, Tuskfish, Moth Wing Eyespot, Juvenile Lemonpeel Angelfish Eyespot) Visual adaptation in avian, insect, and marine life is as varied as the range of species and habitats. The highly developed visual acuity of birds allows them to forage, avoid predators, and adjust for the rapid changes of aerial movement all at once. The changing light levels of the underwater world force much aquatic life to be as dependent on sight for survival as on camouflage morphology such as false eyespots. The insect world also uses eyespots to confuse predators.

It may seem that large wing or body eyespots would attract more attention than desired in a world full of predators, but these ingenious eye-mimicking designs allow for one of nature's most eye-catching means of escape. Although the deception is short lived, the few seconds it buys are just enough for the bug or fish to make its getaway.

Butterflies and Moths

Butterflies have been described as flying flowers, but moths are peerless in their variation of color, pattern, and wing form. Only 24,000 of the 140,000 species of insects with scaly wings are butterflies; the rest are moths. Butterflies are generally day fliers with gaily patterned, colored wings, and they have antennae that end in little knobbed finials. Moths fly at night and usually sport earthy color schemes. They have large furry bodies and plumed feathery antennae.

Ladybirds and Beetles

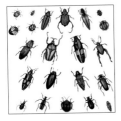

There are over 350,000 known species in the beetle family, compared with 8,600 species of birds and between 4,000 and 5,000 mammals. Beetles thrive everywhere except in the ocean and at the North and South Poles. No other insect has adapted to this planet so successfully. Ladybirds (ladybugs) are a popular member of the beetle family because they are a six-legged alternative to chemical pesticides. They are garden-friendly insects that eat garden pests such as aphids and leaf-dwelling scale insects that threaten orchards, fields, and backyard gardens.

Circle of "Good" Bugs

Insects that produce by-products such as dye, shellac, honey, or silk have historically been considered good bugs because they benefit humankind. For example, about one-third of our diet is the direct result of insect pollination. No insects would mean no oranges, peaches, potatoes, or cotton. They are also the chief architects of many terrestrial ecosystems, creating soil by scavenging and recycling, then becoming food themselves for birds and other beasts in the global food chain.

Black-and-White Fish

Fish, like artists, know that black-and-white stripes make a strong statement. They dress for success in a world where safety is often skin deep. The disruptive coloration of psychedelic stripes and spots breaks up a fish's telltale silhouette to predators. False eyespots mask a fish's real eye and head. When attackers mistakenly go for its tail end, the intended victim flees in the opposite direction. And sometimes bold bands of color help fish identify themselves to their peer species.

Leaf-Eating Bugs

Modern insects have inherited three pairs of jaws from their ancient predecessors that enable them to chew, push, suck, pierce, sponge, or lap food into their mouths. The most successful insects are herbivores, whose species number about 350,000. Some of these vegetarians bore their way into stems of weeds, tree trunks, or root systems, while others use their sharp, hollow mouth parts to tap into plants' vascular systems and sip the sap.

Songbirds

Loud, penetrating song is vital to the songbird's survival in the tangle of branches and leaves where visual displays are largely ineffective. Where songbirds choose to perform often varies according to their feeding niche—in this case the level in the tree canopy where they search for insects.

Cat and Catmint

The flowering herb nepeta, also known as catmint or catnip, has a stimulating effect on most cats. They will brush up against it, roll over it, paw at it, chew it, lick it, leap about, and purr. Cats clearly find this botanical friend a delight and comfort to be around.

Garden of Flowers

Gardens, where nature and civilization meet, reflect our eternal struggle to tame the earth and at the same time savor its endless beauty. Like the refuge of a good friend, a garden shelters us both from the hubbub of human activity and from the rigors of the wilderness. Gardens provide a respite from everyday stresses and a stage for new and different experiences.

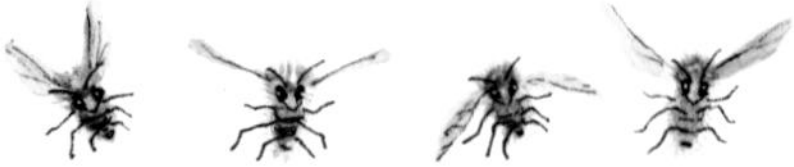